MARY

Mother of Sorrows,
Mother of Defiance

MARY

Mother of Sorrows, Mother of Defiance

Peter Daino, S.M.

ORBIS BOOKS

Maryknoll, New York 10545

The Catholic Foreign Mission Society of America (Maryknoll) recruits and trains people for overseas missionary service. Through Orbis Books, Maryknoll aims to foster the international dialogue that is essential to mission. The books published, however, reflect the opinions of their authors and are not meant to represent the official position of the society.

Published by Orbis Books, Maryknoll, NY 10545
Manufactured in the United States of America

Library of Congress Cataloging-in-Publication Data

Daino, Peter.
    Mary, mother of sorrows, mother of defiance / Peter Daino.
        p.   cm.
    ISBN 0-88344-860-2
    1. Mary, Blessed Virgin, Saint—Meditations.   2. Suffering—
Religious aspects—Catholic Church—Meditations.   3. Christianity
and justice—Catholic Church—Meditations.   4. Catholic Church—
Prayer-books and devotions—English.   I. Title.
BT608.5.D35   1992
248.8'6—dc20   92-34370
                                                          CIP

This book is dedicated to the staff of IMANI who serve destitute mothers and children in Nairobi, and in particular to two recently deceased staff members:

Felix Amina

Clement Njoroge Komu

During their short lives they assisted Mary in her mission, and do so still.

When Herod saw that he had been tricked by the
wise men, he was infuriated, and he sent and killed
all the children in and around Bethlehem who were
two years old or under, according to the time that
he had learned from the wise men. Then was ful-
filled what had been spoken through the prophet
Jeremiah:
"A voice was heard in Ramah,
    wailing and loud lamentation,
Rachel weeping for her children;
    She refused to be consoled,
        because they are no more."
                                        —Matthew 2:16-18

Faith is born out of an infinite loathing for what
makes [people] suffer.
                                        —Albert Camus

For their help in reading the manuscript and offering advice I wish to thank: Joanne Troha, Janelle Sevier, S.N.D., Susan Perry, Robert Ellsberg, Elmer Lange, Johann Roten, S.M., Larry Cada, S.M., Jim Heft, S.M., Bill Behringer, S.M., Frank Damm, S.M., Paula Daino, and Peter Daino, Sr. I wish also to thank the Marianists in Dayton, Philadelphia, Pittsburgh, and Nairobi for their encouragement while I was working on this book. Finally, I wish to thank Marianna Emmanuele, the first coordinator of Maria House, with whom I discussed many sections of this book.

Contents

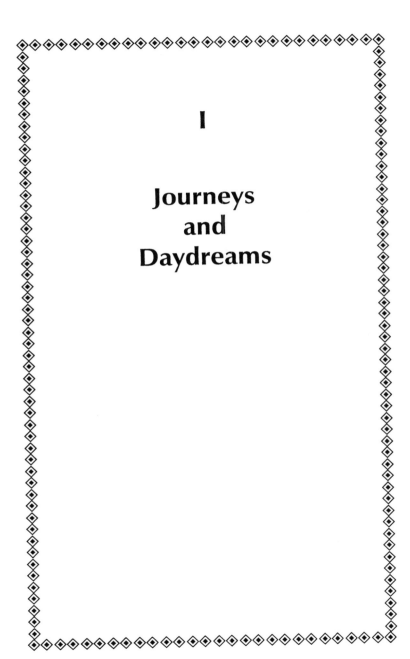

I

Journeys
and
Daydreams

Preface

A Time Apart

I wrote this book during a study year, from June 1989 to June 1990. I was glad for the chance to read more on economics, and Mary. These subjects, diverse as they appear, came together for me as I reflected on my ministry: vocational training and job creation for women.

It was during this study year that I addressed a personal issue: what to do with the grief I carried inside, a grief that had actually changed my facial expression. Friends commented, "You look so distant." Or, "You look so tired." It was neither—only sadness.

The fact is I had been too close to suffering. It had left its smell on me. It had disfigured my face. It had made me bad company.

The suffering wasn't my own. It was the suffering of the women and children in Nairobi's shantytowns. It was the suffering of Njeri, Kamau, Omondi, Omolo, Orick, Maina. Their physical hardships and their pain and their deaths formed a lump of grief inside me, a lump of grief that I carried with me like a tumor.

What was I to do with this grief tumor? That was the personal issue I faced during my year at home. I placed the matter in the hands of Mary. I asked her to be my guide.

What follows is the treatment I received for the tumor. I tell this tale of treatment in the hope that it might help others.

The Marian Axis of Faith

The grief described above is not the same as the grief Elisabeth Kübler-Ross describes in *On Death and Dying*. It does not follow steps of denial and acceptance. How could one ever accept the starvation of children? How could one submit to such an outrage?

This grief of mine, which I began calling apostolic grief, plunged me into a crisis of faith. The death of these children was unacceptable. What should I make of their deaths—and of the world where they could occur? Apostolic grief made me ask the most basic of all questions: Is the universe fundamentally a good place or an evil place?

If Kubler-Ross could not help me with the queries posed by apostolic grief, who could? I read the Gospel. I scoured it for examples of grieving apostles.

And I found one in Mary, the mother of Jesus.

Mary, it seemed to me, must have experienced apostolic grief after the slaughter of the innocents. What did she make of such a senseless massacre? She must have asked herself about the nature of a world where such cruel and inane things are allowed. Apostolic grief must have plunged Mary into a crisis of faith. Much was at stake in the resolution of this crisis. Tremendous spiritual consequences for humankind would ensue from her image of the innocent dead.

In *When Bad Things Happen to Good People,* Rabbi Harold Kushner writes:

Soelle [a contemporary German theologian] . . . suggests that "the most important question we can ask about suffering is whom it serves. Does our suffering serve God or the devil, the cause of becoming alive or being morally paralyzed?" Not, "where does the tragedy come from?" but, "where does it lead?" is the issue on which Soelle would have us focus. In this context she speaks of "the devil's martyrs."

... If the death of an elderly woman in Auschwitz or of a child in a hospital ward leaves us doubting God and less able to affirm the world's goodness, then that woman and that child become "devil's martyrs," witnesses against God, against the meaningfulness of a moral life, rather than witnesses in favor. But (and this is Soelle's most important point) it is not the circumstances of their death that makes them witnesses for or against God. It is our reaction to their death.

... If the death and suffering of someone we love makes us bitter, jealous, against all religion, and incapable of happiness, we turn the person who died into a "devil's martyr."

The massacre of the Bethlehem innocents, I believe, was the crucible event in which Mary's faith was forged. "Whom shall my grief serve?" became the axial question around which Mary's life revolved. Indeed, this was the axial question on which the redemption of the whole world revolved. Would she succumb to bitterness and apostasy? Or would she be a spiritual mentor to Jesus, guiding him through apostolic grief to divine courage? Just as with her answer to the angel Gabriel, so in this matter, too, the angels, the principalities, and the powers of heaven and earth awaited Mary's decision with fear and hope.

Meditation in Motion

On my frequent mission appeal trips to various parishes and dioceses I had a protracted meditation on the massacre of the innocents and Mary's struggle with the devil, who would have liked to make the innocents martyrs for his cause.

My chapel for these meditations on the massacre of the innocents was a 1978 silver Chevy Malibu. It took me to forty different parishes for mission appeals. I drove it, with the radio off, to parishes in Ohio, Michigan, New York, and Pennsylvania.

That car was my cell, my *poustinia*. And yet, I didn't travel alone. A storyteller was with me. In the Spirit, Mary gave me the story, and through the story a new perception of suffering, which I needed to treat the grief tumor inside me.

In the three meditations that follow I focus on three mission appeal trips: Dayton, Ohio, to Mattawan, Michigan; Philadelphia, Pennsylvania, to Syracuse, New York; Pittsburgh, Pennsylvania, to Du Bois, Pennsylvania.

◈ **1** ◈

Massacre in Mattawan

It is ten o'clock on a bright Sunday morning in November. I am standing in front of the parishioners of St. John Bosco Church in Mattawan, Michigan. I arrived in this little village of grape and apple orchards yesterday, after a seven-hour drive from Dayton, Ohio.

Father Bud is introducing me, "the Marianist missionary." He invites me to speak, and I tell my story:

One day a thin, sickly woman in tattered clothing came to Maria House with tiny twins a year old wrapped in rags. Our social worker, Mrs. Mary Wanjau, tried to listen to the distressed mother, but found herself paying more attention to one of the twins, who appeared very dehydrated.

After a few minutes Mrs. Wanjau became so distracted that she suspended the interview, and went off to fetch water for the child. But the child wasn't able to drink it. His breathing became very irregular. At that point Mrs. Wanjau called me. The sound of alarm in her voice made me rush out into the courtyard where the baby was now lying flat on the concrete pavement . . . not breathing at all.

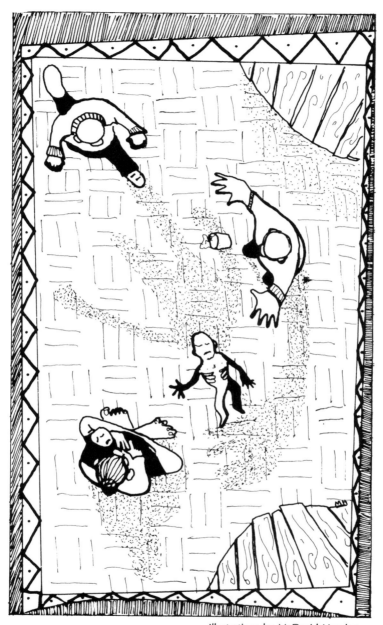

Illustrations by McDavid Henderson

I knelt down beside the dying child and attempted mouth-to-mouth resuscitation. But it was to no avail. The baby only vomited into my mouth some undigested breast milk from his stomach. I couched the little baby's head in my palm, and I looked down at him. What to do?

As I was asking myself what I could do, the child sighed, made a gurgling noise in his throat, turned his head away from my perplexed expression . . . and died.

The purpose of my telling this story to the congregation was to illustrate the hardships of single mothers and their children, the people we were serving at Maria House.

The story was true. It really happened.

Nonetheless, after speaking about this particular incident, I left Mattawan feeling dishonest. I hadn't told the Catholics of Mattawan the whole story.

As I drove through northeast Indiana on my way south to Ohio's Route 75, I prayed to Mary. I told her about the lump of grief I felt. I asked her for healing.

The healing came in the form of a story. Driving along the autumn highways of Indiana, I had a daydream, a daydream that peopled the inside of my silver Chevy with unexpected sojourners.

. . . It is early morning. Many residents of Bethlehem are still sleeping. Mary is alone, drawing water from a small well at the edge of town.

She hears footsteps! Many hundreds of footsteps! The sound of soldiers marching!

Mary is alarmed. She looks in the direction of the noise. She sees a cloud of dust in the distance. She remembers Joseph's dream. This cloud might portend the evil he had described to her.

Mary drops the water skins. She runs to her house. Barely through the front door, she hears the first cries for help. She scurries onto the roof. Looking toward the commotion, she sees unkempt soldiers emerge from the cloud of dust. Soldiers from the king's court.

The soldiers round up mothers and infants. Some of the infants are drowsy with sleep. Others are shrieking uncontrollably. Forty bewildered women with infants in their arms are herded into the center of the village square and made to stand there in the chilled air.

The armed men form a circle around the defenseless women; with hairy arms they unsheathe their iron swords from leather scabbards. In unison the soldiers point their swords to the sky. They make a military howl and curse and yelp like jackals . . . and then move in on their captives.

The women resist. They hiss and scream at the soldiers. They tear at the eyes of the Romans.

But the women are quickly overpowered and pushed violently to the stone pavement.

The soldiers push their weapons into the unprotected bodies of the newborn boys. Some of the infants die while still clinging to their mothers. Others are torn away from their mothers, lifted up, hurled with sporting gestures to the ground, and slaughtered on the pavement by the laughing soldiers.

Mary, still standing on the rooftop, suddenly feels a hand on her shoulder. She jumps, terrified.

It's only Joseph. He takes her by the arm and hurries her down off the roof and into the kitchen. Joseph's pupils dilate; his nostrils flare. ''Thank God you weren't seen! Mary, we must flee at once!''

Mary shakes her head in disagreement. ''What about our neighbors? We can't abandon them.''

Joseph grips her at the waist and looks into her eyes. ''Listen, if we stay here it is certain death for Jesus. There is nothing we can do now for our neighbors. Come! Come! We must get away.''

Mary gasps. She tilts her head back, and, like a drowning

woman, lifts her mouth higher, struggling for air. She closes her
eyes and shakes her head again.

At that moment the kitchen door swings open. It's Deborah,
a neighbor. Panting, she yells, "Flee! Oh, flee! Flee now! My
child's body still lies on the village pavement. But I've rushed
here to make you leave. Go! Go, now!"

Deborah fixes her eyes on Mary. She waits for an answer.

Mary tightens her fist. She bites her lip. "All right then. Let
us go, Joseph. By the south road. And God help us!"

Satisfied, Deborah turns to exit. She blows out the flames of
the menorah on her way out the kitchen door, saying, "Why
bother with silly hope? There is no reason any more to keep
the candles lit."

The baby Jesus is crying, frightened by the clamor outside.
His mother hushes him. She wraps him in many blankets so
that he appears to be a larger, older child. To a casual onlooker,
he appears to be four or five years old. If ordered to remove
the blankets, she will say the child is a leper and contagious.

They rush out of the backyard gate. With Mary and the child
mounted on the donkey, Joseph engineers the daring escape.
He drags the sleepy animal by its reins. Racing down the narrow
streets of Bethlehem, he yanks the reluctant donkey faster than
the stubborn beast cares to go. Mary and her infant are almost
thrown off when the donkey takes a tight corner near the syn-
agogue.

Fortunately, Joseph knows all the back alleys and the hidden
passages of his hometown. He gets his family to the south gate
of the village undetected. Thank God, no sentry has been posted
there. The hunted family dashes under the arch and out the
portal. Free!

Joseph does not allow the donkey to ease his canter until
they are half a day's journey away from Bethlehem. It is getting
dark. But the dark holds less terror than the road behind them.
So on they trek until sunrise the next day. At last they enter the
desert of Sinai.

And there . . . there in the quiet, enigmatic desert, Mary is tempted. In the desert she is tried. There, in that place where Jesus will struggle thirty years later, the tempter makes his first attempt to sabotage the divine project. The Silencer tries to lose the Mother of Redemption in the desert void. The Silencer, that evil voice of fatalism within the bereaved, tries to induce Mary into a state of surrender and resignation.

"Of course, I'm grateful my child escaped alive. But the carnage, the iron swords, the baby blood, the red pavement stones, and the empty look of mothers in shock. What do I feel about this? A jealous king—that's nothing new. A massacre of boys under two—well, what else do you expect from a jealous king who feels threatened? It's all unfortunate, but that's reality. Nothing can be done about it. A person can't beat the system. It is better to forget and feel nothing."

Mary is lured by these thoughts of capitulation. She has a great desire to live mute in the middle of the silent Sinai.

Oh, deafness come!
Muteness, my ally
in this wasteland,
numb my feelings.
Let me go blank.

Different options for the pain come to Mary. The Silencer puts thoughts of escape in her mind: "I could dull this troublesome heart with drink or drugs—just become apathetic. Nothing really matters anyway. I could be stoic—bear with it and grin. I could feign a fiat to fatalism, 'I accept, I accept' . . . anything to avoid feeling again."

The temptation lasts for several days. It follows her on the desert road.

Then one night, still in the Sinai, Mary sits down on the cool, sandy ground and leans her aching back against a withered desert shrub. She remains motionless for hours as she looks

across the vast emptiness and ponders a question.

She ponders and ponders the same question: Whom does my grief serve?

And then she speaks into the noiseless dark:

"Stop your pacing, sister Rachel,
Here, come to me, sit down.

Your hand in mine, sister Rachel,
Weep, lament, break silence.

The Silencer, sister Rachel,
Quells your cry of protest.

He wants fiat, sister Rachel,
Defy him! Refuse your fiat!

Don't accept it, sister Rachel,
Don't bear it with a grin.

Whom will it serve, sister Rachel,
If you mutely submit?

Wail, mourn aloud, sister Rachel,
Feel, feel all your feelings.

Unleash grief's force, sister Rachel,
To change what made you grieve.

Unleash grief's force, sister Rachel,
The mighty to bring down.

Unleash grief's force, sister Rachel,
The wealthy to chase out.

Raise the lowly, sister Rachel,
Feed the hungry. Rise up!

Of your child you are deprived,
Let no one steal your rage."

With these words to her bereaved sisters, Mary rips apart the Silencer's web. She makes her way out of the bonds of muteness. She knows now what to do with her grief. She knows now whom her grief will serve. And so, she removes a small container from her garment and scoops a handful of desert sand into it. She vows that some day she will return to Bethlehem and bury the innocent dead.

Finally, Mary begins to cry. She weeps profusely. The sword of sorrow, foretold by Simeon, pierces her through. She gasps, "It hurts!" She wails aloud: "Oh! God, it hurts!"

The Silencer withdraws. How he hates to hear crying. And worse yet, he hates to hear people lament to God. Any talking to God undermines the strategy of the Silencer.

2

Requiem in Syracuse

It is a snowy Sunday morning in early March. I am sitting in the sanctuary of Our Lady of Pompei Church in Syracuse, New York. I arrived in this Italian American neighborhood yesterday, after driving six hours from Philadelphia, Pennsylvania. Our Lady of Pompei parish is "home" to me. My father grew up here. My grandparents, uncles, and aunts used to tell me stories about the "Nort-a-side."

I have just finished giving my mission appeal. Now the collection is being taken up by the ushers. I wonder what the congregation thinks of the story about the dehydrated child who died at Maria House. How would they have reacted to such a death?

My mind wanders. I remember another snowy morning in this parish, at Assumption Cemetery. It was early December 1969.

. . . "Frank, I won't leave you!" shouts my grandmother. She stands stubbornly in a foot of snow. Her husband's coffin has just been blessed and interred in a mausoleum, awaiting burial come the spring thaw. The ceremony is over. But Grandma Daino refuses to budge. She keeps vigil beside the man she loved and battled for fifty years, crying and wailing.

The priest and his altar boys are already gone; they're off to the next funeral. But Grandma will not leave Assumption Cemetery. My father and his brothers are trying to coax her over to the car. She shouts the louder, "Frank, I'll never leave you. I'm staying here with you."

Finally, one of my widowed aunts comes forward and takes my grandmother by the elbow. "Come along, Lily, get into the car," she says, "you're not leaving Frank."

And she didn't. Every day of her life after my grandfather died, for eleven years, Grandma said a rosary for Frank. Sitting in a large armchair, this little Sicilian lady could be seen slouching over to one side, leaning against one of the armrests, dangling her rosary so that it touched the carpet, each bead tapping the ground—*pater, pater,* knock, knock—to signal my grandfather that he was not forgotten.

Grandma knew how to lament. Her beads dropped like noisy tears on the ground—*ave, ave,* I miss you—one after another, day after day. The first couple of years she would skip the Gloria and punctuate the end of a decade with, "Oh, Frank."

Sitting in Our Lady of Pompei Church this winter morning, I feel grateful. I say so, in prayer, to Grandma, whose body is now buried beside the body of her Frank. I thank her because I see now what she was doing. With that rosary in hand she became a companion of the *Mater Dolorosa.* Grandma did, indeed, stay with Frank, though not where she left him. Grief never leaves you where it finds you . . .

Sitting in Our Lady of Pompei Church this winter morning, I thank Mary for the rosary, the language of my grandmother's grief. I thank Mary for being my grandmother's mentor in the strange language of grief. What an odd language, indeed, this language of grief, a language of remembering, of lament, and at the same time, in a mysterious way, also the language of confident anticipation, opening one to those who live in the future.

After the last mass I say goodbye to the recently appointed pastor of Our Lady of Pompei parish, Father Mirabito, get into my Chevy "chapel" and head south on Route 81. I drive through the gorgeous whited hills of New York's Southern Tier. By the time I get to the Wilkes-Barre entrance to the Pennsylvania Turnpike, I am deep in a daydream, and I find the car peopled again. The sojourners have returned to teach me the language of grief.

... *"I almost lost my mind. Three days made me fear the worst. And look at your muddy prayer shawl!" Mary walks slowly now. She wants to take in all Jesus is telling her.*

"I got tangled up, all right." The twelve-year-old is smiling, obviously happy to be with his family again.

"What was your first reaction?" Mary asks.

"When I found the body, I felt ill. But the response of the soldier surprised me."

"Why? What did he do?"

"It wasn't so much what he did. It was the matter-of-fact tone in his voice." Jesus looks ahead at the dirt road that wiggles down the hill of Jerusalem.

"What did he say?" Mary asks.

"He told me to remove the shawl and to surrender the body. He said that this was a routine matter—I should not get involved. The government would bury the corpse."

Mary raises her eyebrows. "Did you believe him?"

"Why not?"

Mary stops walking and pulls Jesus to the side of the road. "What do you think the child died from?"

"Hunger," says Jesus.

"And what is the cause of the hunger?" Mary asks.

"The occupation?" Jesus is unsure.

Jaw tightened and extended, Mary says, "We have been exporting food to Rome for decades now while our people languish."

"The soldier admitted the child's death was truly sad. He told me, 'Things like that happen.' "

Mary doesn't say a word. Pilgrims pass by, hurrying down the hill.

Jesus continues, "The soldier told me, 'If you want to survive in this world, keep quiet and look the other way.' "

"Then they detained you for three days?"

"Yes," Jesus says, "to educate me."

"About what?" Mary's eyes narrow.

"Occupation philosophy," Jesus answers.

"What's that?"

"It's a kind of stoicism. One doesn't make so much fuss about a discovered corpse. I ought to have reported it and left the rest to the authorities." The twelve-year-old looks up at his mother with a confused expression on his face.

"What in your behavior," she asks, "offended them?"

"I should not have cried out," Jesus says. "They didn't like all the noise."

"What else?" Mary asks.

"Holding the dead child was bad enough," Jesus answers, "but wanting to bury the child and wrapping the corpse in my shawl was completely out of order and none of my business."

"And what is the proper response to the death of the inno-cent according to occupation philosophy?" Mary demands.

"Indifference."

Mary has never told Jesus about the events surrounding their exile in Egypt. He only knows that the family lived there for a couple of years before returning to establish a home in Naza-reth.

She has been afraid to tell him. Not that she feels easy about hiding things from him. In fact, she has struggled for ten years over whether or not to tell him. She wants to protect him.

But losing Jesus for three days occasions a new round of debate on the issue. How will the news of the atrocity affect Jesus? Will it make him morbid? Angry? Will he become pes-simistic about humankind? What impact will this news have on the formation of his character?

"Let's keep walking," Mary says. Mother and son descend the hill. Neither speaks.

Mary continues to ponder: "Things like that happen," "Rou-tine matter," "Keep quiet." Mary hates these statements of the soldier. She recognizes the Silencer.

"Occupation philosophy," "Look the other way," "None of your business." "Yes," she says to herself, "this is all very famil-iar."

Mary decides. "I'm going to tell him. I must tell him, so that he learns to spot the Silencer."

She speaks. "We are not going back to Nazareth today. We are taking a side trip."

"What about Father?" Jesus asks.

"He has business to finish at home. He will go ahead of us to Nazareth. We will see him there the day after tomorrow. I

am sending a message to the front of the caravan where he is walking with friends—probably talking with them about your ordeal. Now, let's take our leave.''

They part company with the caravan and strike off in an eastward direction. With her son at her side, Mary walks quickly and with determination toward Bethlehem. Her face is defiant; her jaw set like flint.

Mary tells Jesus about the dust cloud and about dropping the water skins. She tells him about running home. She tries to tell him about what she saw from the rooftop.

''Your playmates . . . I mean . . . the children under two years old . . . I mean . . . well . . . my son, I don't know how to tell you this.''

Jesus waits. He listens.

Mary gets angry. ''No one should have to say what I am saying to you today, and no one should have to listen to it.''

Jesus is quiet.

''I really don't know how to tell you about this, but you are the sole survivor of a massacre that took place ten years ago in Bethlehem.'' Mary looks up at the sky. She shakes her head.

''What?'' Jesus is incredulous.

''I did not think human beings were capable of such brutality. But I saw it myself. Roman soldiers came and slaughtered forty infants your age, and you are the only one who escaped.'' Her voice cracks. She speaks about the massacre as if it happened only an hour ago. The event is close to her, consuming her. There is wetness and rage in her eyes.

''I would like to know more.'' The twelve-year-old has a stunned expression on his face.

''Would you like to go to their grave?'' Mary asks.

"Yes."

"And after that," says Mary, "I'd like you to visit one of the mothers who lost a child in the massacre."

After a day's journey they reach Bethlehem. Mary takes Jesus directly to the children's grave. There is a cluster of young trees, about ten years old, erect as tomb markers. The setting sun is at eye level, and it is casting long shadows around the spot where the survivors stand.

Mary reaches for Jesus. She holds his hand firmly. "A child's death is something to get angry about, my son. You should not keep quiet. It is not routine, and I do not want you ever to look the other way."

Jesus looks with admiration at this woman.

"None of your business?" Mary squeezes his hand tightly. "Your Father's business is justice, and you must be about your Father's business."

She releases his hand. All is still. After a few minutes Mary proceeds with a strange litany.

"Jacob," she shouts and adds, "Never again!"

"Aaron," she shouts and adds, "Never again!"

"Tobias," she shouts and adds, "Never again!"

Mary announces each child's name from memory and adds, "Never again!"

Then she removes a small container from her garment and, while slowly emptying its contents of sand over the mass grave, repeats verses from the Book of Lamentations, words that seem as familiar to her as water and salt.

> Worn out from weeping are my eyes,
> within me all is in ferment;

My gall is poured out on the ground
  because of the downfall of the daughter of
    my people,
As child and infant faint away
  in the open spaces of the town.

They ask their mothers,
  "Where is the cereal?"—in vain,
As they faint away like the wounded
  in the streets of the city,
And breathe their last
  in their mother's arms.

Lamentations 2:11, 12

Jesus' sobs choke him. He can't swallow. He is gasping for
air. Mary stands beside him and holds him up. She teaches God
to grieve.

"Try breathing this way. Yes, that's better. Now, pray with
me: 'Cry out to the Lord . . .'"

Jesus continues the verse:

    . . . Moan, O daughter Zion!
Let your tears flow like a torrent
    day and night;
Let there be no respite for you,
    no repose for your eyes.
Rise up, shrill in the night,
    at the beginning of every watch;
Pour out your heart like water
    in the presence of the Lord;
Lift up your hands to God
    for the lives of your little ones.

Lamentations 2:18, 19

After praying in this fashion, mother and son remain quiet for another hour. Then Jesus goes off to speak with one of the bereaved mothers. Mary stays behind at the gravesite that night and keeps vigil.

Soft light from the menorah candles makes shadows around the empty dishes. The room is redolent with the scent of bread, onions, and olive oil.

". . . And the dust cloud disappeared long before the wailing did." Rachel concludes her decription of the massacre.

"Tell me," Jesus says, "about your life since then."

"It has been slow going. I have sometimes felt mute, and at other times I have lamented and complained to God. But I am happiest when I work. I suppose you could call my different states of mind the phases of grief. But it isn't quite as clean as that. It is hard to describe."

"Please, try," Jesus insists.

"When it first happened I was speechless. I did not want to be around people. I wanted to feel it. I couldn't. I wanted the hurt to come so I might heal. But nothing happened. No tears. I was numb."

"And then?"

"I began to pray. And slowly my feelings returned. Sometimes I shouted. Often I wept. That is how I got the name, Rachel."

"I see."

"Yes," continues Rachel, "the tears came after the numbness. And, for me, it was like rain after a long drought. The most important thing is that I was able to talk to God again. Though, admittedly, all I did was complain."

"How long did this go on?"

"Until," says Rachel, "I was able to light the menorah candles again."

"Oh?"

"Right after the massacre I extinguished the candles at your mother's house. For many years I could not light the candles."

Rachel pauses.

"But after months of lamentation, and after all my complaining to God, for some reason, I began lighting the candles again. I can't explain why, or precisely when I started feeling different."

"What is this different feeling?" Jesus asks.

"Courage." Rachel looks intently at Jesus.

"I want to defy the darkness—the dark, silent force of resignation. And so, I light the candles, and I tell the story."

"What do others do to defy that silencing force?"

"Your mother's form of defiance is what I call the 'intrepid return.' "

"What do you mean," Jesus says.

"She comes out of Egypt. Like Moses she crosses the Red Sea. In this act of defiance she marches against Caesar and Herod and all the 'mighty on their thrones.' She returns with the hunted king."

Jesus ponders.

"Visiting the grave of the innocents," Rachel continues, "is another example of your mother's defiance. She returns to the site of the massacre. She remembers."

Jesus looks out the window toward the gravesite where Mary is keeping vigil. He recalls his mother's necrology of "never again."

"There are deaths," Rachel says, "that scandalize us. We don't want to remember these deaths. We don't want to hear the names of people who have died these deaths. There are deaths that are so stupid, and so pointless . . . and so, so useless that . . ." Rachel vigorously wipes her eyes with both fists. She bites on her lower lip and knits her brow. She waits until her voice returns.

Looking out the window into the moonless night, she continues, "Such deaths make me wonder whether my life, or your life, or any life is just a chance event. Such deaths make me wonder whether my existence, any existence, is a random, meaningless chemical accident. Is it that we live in a universe that is basically a stupid, stupid place? That is the question my grief poses, and that is why grief is so much like fear."

Jesus listens, deep in thought.

"So you see, dear child, if we keep silent, if we never speak the names of the innocent dead, we are no longer just wondering whether the universe is a stupid place. If we keep silent about such inane deaths then we are admitting that, indeed, the universe is a stupid place and nothing better can be expected of it."

Rachel stands up and walks toward the burning candles. "When we keep silent about the victims of atrocity, such as our Bethlehem infants, then we turn these victims of atrocity into martyrs for the devil, martyrs for despair and disbelief."

Rachel gently places her hand at the base of the menorah. "Your mother gave this to me. She is the one who helped me to understand all that I am telling you tonight. She has been my guide through the phases of grief. She is the mentor of the defiant."

The boy Jesus looks up at Rachel and notices how beautiful she is in the soft glow of the candle flame. He puts his wet palms together and says, "Tell me, shall I too pass through these phases of grief?"

"You have already started. Mary and you recited lamentation prayers together, and you cried. Thank God for those tears. They came to you swiftly."

"And what about defiance?" asks Jesus.

"You will learn first what defiance is not. You will learn that defiance is not obstinacy, or hatred, or violence."

"What is it then?" Jesus asks.

"It is taking a stand, a stand for the Reign of Heaven, all the while loving those you oppose."

"And what will this cost me?"

"Everything."

Neither speaks for several minutes. Then Jesus sighs and nods his head slowly, as if saying yes to some unspoken request. He gets up to go.

Rachel moves over to him and grasps the boy's left shoulder with her muscular hand. "I have waited many years to meet you, the sole survivor. Remember, my dear child, that all your playmates who died in this village live on in you. Make them martyrs for God. In this world gone wrong, put things right."

She pauses and takes a deep breath.

"I do not understand why this world is so full of grief. But that is not the most helpful question one can ask about grief. No, no. The most helpful question one can ask about grief, your mother asked me many years ago. Now I ask you: 'Whom will your grief serve?' "

Jesus stares at Rachel for a long while. He walks over to the burning candles, lifts the menorah from the table and places his still dirty prayer shawl as an altar cloth beneath it.

"Thank you, and farewell," he says, walking out the door, "I must be about my Father's business."

3

Defiance in Du Bois

It is a rainy Sunday morning—June 23, 1990, to be precise. My study year in the United States is almost over. This 11:15 A.M. gathering of the parish of St. Catherine in Du Bois, Pennsylvania, is one of the last congregations that I will address before my return to Africa. I drove here yesterday from Pittsburgh, a four-hour trip north to northeast. Over the last three seasons my sermon has evolved.

We are often told that Mary said *"fiat"* at the foot of the cross. But I don't believe it! I cannot imagine her nodding her head in submission: "O God, I accept this atrocity."

Rather, if we are to put any words from her earlier life on the lips of the *Stabat Mater,* they would be, I am sure, from the Magnificat: "God will bring down the mighty from their thrones, and exalt the lowly; God will chase away the rich, and feed the hungry."

Not resigned, not stoic, or fatalistic, Mary, the outraged mother, is defiant at the foot of the cross. The *fiat* of the incarnation has become, at the crucifixion, a *defiat.* Mary says, "NO!" at the foot of the cross.

And she still says no today at the foot of the cross. She still sings the Magnificat there.

Today, while I am speaking to you, there are children walking the streets of Nairobi looking for food in garbage dumpsters. Mary stands at the foot of their cross and cries out, "Let the mighty be brought down from their thrones, and let these lowly ones be exalted. . . . For God's sake, let the hungry be given food!"

To forty thousand children a day dying of malnutrition and preventable disease Mary cries, "No!"

It is not "*fiat*" that Mary speaks at the foot of the cross. It is "*defiat*," defiance, Magnificat.

At the foot of the cross Mary took a stand. She stood up against all that brought down her child. She still stands up today, against all political, social, and economic systems that victimize children.

When I finish this sermon, I sit down. As the hymn at the Presentation of the Gifts is played I think, "Peter, that is not the way to raise money. They won't like what you've said." But I feel satisfied nonetheless. I've come a long way since Mattawan.

I bid farewell to Father Brugger and thank him for the collection, which in fact was quite large, and drive west on Route 80, then south on Route 79. While driving through the wooded hills of western Pennsylvania, the now familiar sojourners join me. It is their last chance to put me right before I go back to Kenya. In an early summer daydream, I find Mary and Rachel keeping vigil at the tomb of Jesus on the first Holy Saturday.

. . . The day after Passover Mary and Rachel are standing at Jesus' gravesite. Off to their left, at a distance, are two Roman soldiers.

Mary and Rachel hear the two men talking.

"The defiant one now lies in the tomb. What did his efforts come to? Whom did his suffering serve?" The standing guard

spits on the ground and stares at the large stone covering the entrance to the sepulchre.

"Well, let him rest now in Roman peace," says the other guard, squatting in front of the stone. He rolls a pair of dice.

"At least Herod's son finished his father's business," says the standing guard.

"What's that?" The squatting guard is distracted by his two of a kind and rubs the dice appreciatively.

"Herod's son finished the job of slaughtering the innocents. This fellow got away the first time, but now he's one more foolish martyr. Yes, one more martyr for hell." The standing guard laughs, spits again, and turns his back to the stone.

Rachel sighs and turns toward Mary.

"I sold Jesus a bill of goods." Rachel pounds her fist and purses her lips, enraged.

"Wait. Come here and sit down." Mary leads Rachel to the shade of a cedar tree. They both sit down on its gnarled, exposed roots. "Now, what are you saying?"

"I told your son that he would be able to put things right; that he could make a difference; I said that his defiance would set free the innocent dead." Rachel shakes her head and looks down at the dry, baked soil. "How naive I was."

Mary reaches over and puts her hand under Rachel's chin and lifts up the remorseful woman's downcast face. "Look at me," says Mary, "I had a dream last night. And I saw hell collapse. I saw Jesus, his jaw set like flint, crash the gates of hell."

"But all I see here is a tomb and some guards," says Rachel.

"Appearances deceive," Mary says. "The Romans have set a seal of imperial control on the tomb of Jesus. But do the Romans rule the next world? There, indeed, their proud empire ends."

"What are you saying?"

"Even as they guard his tomb," Mary explains, "the actual ruler of the living and the dead is crashing through the gates of hell, bolted for centuries by a force greater than this Roman guard. While his own tomb is sealed tight, Christ unseals the tombs of everyone else. He harrows hell."

Mary's face is beaming with an uncommon light. She exults in the Spirit and proclaims:

"Oh, see the King of glory enters,
carrying his cross.

Look, the escaped innocent enters
the sad yaw of hell.

He passes hell's gate; the dead awake,
yes, surprised by joy.

A glad sound breaks in that noiseless place;
hark, 'Alleluia!'

The Silencer sits disconsolate,
covering his ears."

"And in your dream," asks Rachel, "did you see the innocents? What happens to them?"

"Jesus calls them each by name," says Mary as she continues her story with a cadence and rhythm of one in ecstasy:

"Then to make the final insult to hell,
that sole survivor

Recites the names of the innocents,
each shouted aloud.

And those names shatter the awe-ful silence.
Thus, Christ harrows hell."

"What happens after that?" Rachel asks.

"An unusual conversation," says Mary.

"Who speaks?" inquires Rachel.

"In this dream of mine, after Jesus descends into hell and after he speaks the names of the innocent dead, I hear Jesus speak with . . ."—Mary has a quizzical look on her face—"with Herod."

"Those sound like Hebrew names."

"Yes, they are," says Jesus.

"I once lived in Judah."

"Yes, I know," says Jesus.

"How?"

"Because I also lived there," says Jesus.

"And who are you?"

"I am the escaped innocent," says Jesus.

"What?"

"I am the sole survivor of the massacre you ordered at Bethlehem."

"I never ordered such a massacre. At least I don't remember doing it. Oh, wait, maybe I did. Were these pretenders to the throne?"

"They were babies at the breast," says Jesus.

"Oh, well, why are you looking for them here?"

"I'm not," says Jesus.

"So why did you call out their names?"

"In order to harrow hell," says Jesus.

"Harrow hell?"

"When I call out the names of the innocent victims of atrocity," says Jesus, *"and damn the cause of their death, it harrows hell."*

"And so you have called out the names of the victims of the Bethlehem slaughter, and now you will damn me, the one who ordered them slaughtered?"

"No, Herod, I have not come to damn you. I have come that you might have life."

"Then who have you come to damn?"

"The Silencer," says Jesus.

"What's that?"

"It is what keeps you here in hell. It is what entraps everyone who believes that nothing can be done about evil. It is that hideous force in human hearts that makes people believe injustice and malice are inevitable." Jesus continues in a determined voice, *"Herod, human history is not fixed. There need not be another slaughter ever again. It can stop. If only the human race would defy the Silencer, and believe the Good News."*

"And what is the Good News?" asks Herod.

"The Good News is that one child survived your order. And that child was taught to defy the power of human indifference — to break the Silence! This child grew up to be a prophet who taught people to speak their minds. And then this sole survivor of your massacre was finally apprehended and crucified."

"Well, that goes to show you — there is no vindication for the righteous," Herod laughs.

Jesus interrupts him. "This escaped innocent crucified, who descends into hell, now ascends to God's Kingdom to open the wedding banquet there for all your victims."

Herod does not know what else to say. He moves away.

"That's all I saw in the dream," Mary said in conclusion. "I don't know if Herod ever came back to Jesus."

Listening to Mary and watching the expressive features of her shining face have calmed Rachel. Unclenching her fists and opening her hands, she kneels down now in front of Mary, and begs for a blessing.

Mary places her palms firmly on Rachel's head. She prays:

> *"Woman, suffering woman,*
> *Sing, 'Alleluia.'*
>
> *Be now a herald of good news.*
> *The table is turned.*
>
> *Mighty Herod is brought down;*
> *The lowly arise;*
>
> *Every wrong is put right!*
> *Our Redeemer lives!*
>
> *Mama, suffering mama,*
> *Your labor is shared*
>
> *By the Suffering Servant,*
> *The Defiant One,*
>
> *From the labor of his death*
> *A new race is born."*

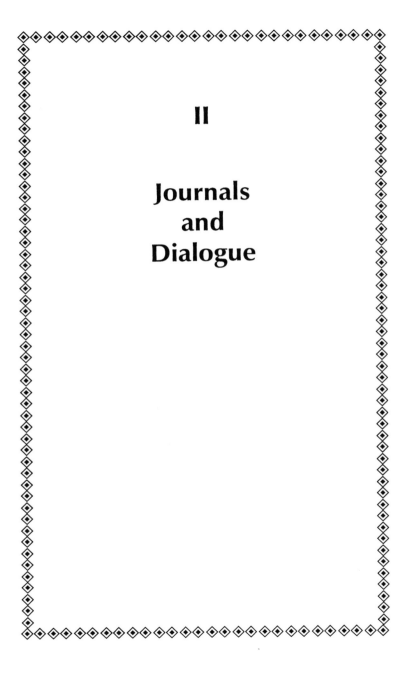

II

Journals
and
Dialogue

Preface

The study year of 1989-1990 was not an academic exercise for me. Something dear was at stake. There were two forces struggling in me, contesting for ownership of my grief.

One of the two forces I call the Silencer. The Silencer is that insidious force that tempts me to detour the grieving process through a perverted form of stoic surrender: "Better to forget this; there is nothing else I can do."

But such stoic surrender is dishonest! Worse yet, it makes martyrs for the devil—it weakens our faith in the outcome of the human project. And this is precisely what the Silencer wants.

The Silencer abhors funerals and burials. He hates the sound of weeping and lamentation. The Silencer suggests to bereaved people that they avoid the pain and omit the mourning. "What difference does it make?" the Silencer whispers.

But this attitude deprives me of the one choice I still have as a bereaved person.

Life, whether I like it or not, is painful. The one choice I still have in the matter is whether to make my pain meaningful or meaningless.

The question is not "whether" life hurts, but how to take life's hurt and change it into holy defiance.

The Silencer does everything in his power to keep this change from happening. He tries to subvert the process of grief. He wants me to waste this spiritual resource, because he knows that wasted grief maintains the status quo. Every time grief is wasted, a word of protest is aborted. And this, to the Silencer's delight, keeps things just as they are.

The Holy Spirit opposes the Silencer. The Holy Spirit, St. Paul says, helps the bereaved to groan.

The Spirit helps me to grieve, gives me release and expression for my sorrow. The Spirit does this in a variety of ways. One of these ways is Mary. She, the one Simeon predicted would be pierced by the sword of sorrow, helps me to lament, helps me to comfort others. Through the *Mater Dolorosa* I am able to tap the spiritual resources of grief.

Mary takes me on a journey. She leads me through the phases of grief, as once she led Jesus. And at appropriate intervals, she asks me this question:

> "Whom will your grief serve?
> Will it serve the cause of Heaven
> or the cause of Silence?"

Mary does not try to make apologies for God or explain away the existence of suffering. She is not contending that this is the best of all possible worlds. She is not preaching a theodicy. She does not ask the "why" of suffering; rather, Mary asks "how." And "how" always implies a choice.

Mary addresses the bereaved in these words: "Either you join your grief to the mystery of God's suffering in Christ for the cause of goodness, love, and truth—the Reign of Heaven; or you let your grief serve the opposite cause of bitterness, envy, and despair—the Reign of the Silencer."

That's Mary's question: "Whom does your grief serve?"

My mission-appeal trips and daydreams were changing me. These changes were reflected in my journals—journals in which I talk with Mary about my sermons in Mattawan, Syracuse, and Du Bois.

What follows are three different dialogues that correspond with those three sermons. The journals were written in the autumn, the winter, and the spring.

◈ **4** ◈

The Autumn Journal

"I didn't tell the whole story at Mattawan."

"Yes," says Mary, "that's right."

"I am ashamed of the ending."

"It is all right not to tell a Sunday congregation the ending of the story. But," Mary says, "do now tell me."

"The child died in the courtyard of Maria House. The mother and I and the surviving twin went with his body immediately to Kenyatta National Hospital. The part I left out of the sermon took place at the Kenyatta emergency room. Here is what happened . . ."

"I can take care of that for you, if you like." The nurse seems so serene.

"Can you give us a minute?" I say.

I look down at the body of the child cradled in my arms. He is smaller than most boys a year old. He probably never had a full stomach in his short life—a life that ended fifty minutes ago.

"What about a funeral?" asks his mother.

Looking around the emergency room and seeing scores of children in various stages of distress, I remember two squatter children whose funerals I never attended. One, an infant, had died when a piece of plastic roof covering the family shack had fallen on him, smothering him in his sleep. The other, a toddler, had died during an outbreak of cholera. I muse on the importance of burial rites in Africa.

"What would you like to do with the body?" The nurse has returned to the emergency room bench where we are seated.

"Sorry, we haven't yet decided," I say.

"I'll give you time." The nurse nods to the mother and hurries off.

"What about a funeral?" the mother asks again.

"You are barely surviving yourself. And look at your remaining twin. She is very sick." I look down, stare at the linoleum floor, and think:

The little girl is very sick. Both she and her mother are dressed in rags and haven't eaten for days. They have no place to sleep but the streets. What they need is medical attention, food, and some kind of accommodation. I can telephone the Missionary Sisters of Charity, who run a shelter for the indigent and everything will be taken care of. Let me do this for her. But I'm not bringing her back here to hassle with the mortuary and all that red tape. It would also take days to get a cemetery plot and a casket. Forget it. I know what I'm doing. There is nothing else that can be done for this dead boy.

I turn to the mother, "Let the hospital take care of it." I look away and add, "I don't think a funeral will be necessary."

The mother stiffly nods her head in resignation, and says, "It doesn't matter."

"There we are," says the nurse as I hand her the boy's body. "We'll take care of this right away. It happens all the time. No sense in making a fuss."

We didn't.

I look over at the mother and she looks at me. We can't say a word. The silence is too heavy.

"That's the part I leave out of my sermons."

"Yes," Mary says.

"Silence is not always golden," I say.

"I agree," Mary states. "Sometimes it is yellow."

◈ **5** ◈

The Winter Journal

"You taught my grandmother the language of grief. You, *Mater Dolorosa,* helped her overcome muteness. Now, please, teach me."

"First," says Mary, "describe for me this muteness you speak of."

"It's hell," I say.

"Go on," says Mary. "What, for you, is hell?"

"Hell," I say, "happens when one gives up fighting and feeling. Hell happens when one is fettered by resignation."

"Did it take you long to notice you were in hell?" she asks.

"Yes," I say, "because everything seemed so normal."

"Normal?"

"Of course," I say. "Many cool, calm, collected people, all having a nice day are in hell. We're even smiling, or to be more precise, we're grinning. A grin goes no deeper than the lips."

"Living in hell," says Mary, "must require a lot of emotional control."

"What do you mean?" I say.

"I mean that despair takes a lot of effort."

"Please explain," I insist.

"You wanted to speak to the *Mater Dolorosa,* and I am speaking to you. I know something about hell. And I can tell you that I am not welcome there. You see, sorrow is not allowed in hell. Sorrow is the opposite of despair. That is why crying is not permitted. Crying would undermine everything."

"Why?"

"Emotional control," she repeats the words, "is the key to living in hell. Being subdued and overly polite are the virtues you'll need."

I don't respond. I consider her point.

She continues: "No vulgarity can be heard in hell. Not even the name of the place is spoken. Everything would be ruined if someone were to say, 'Oh hell!' Decorum is the rule. No shouting, please. Weeping and gnashing of teeth would be most improper. I sometimes wonder if that is why Jesus recommended that the hell-fettered weep and gnash their teeth. A protest would undo hell. It would be heresy. Acceptance, you see, is the religion of hell."

"But, *Dolorosa,* I do not accept. And I would like to cry out. . . . Please, help me escape from hell."

"Listen to me," she says. "Despite the atrocities you've witnessed—the child who died of suffocation, the other who died of cholera, and the most recent one who died of hunger— despite the seeming victory of evil over innocence, you must not say to yourself that nothing can change."

"Why not?" I ask.

"Those words," she says, "create martyrs for the devil. Saying them makes a person numb and hell-bound."

"So, tell me, who can rescue us from the hell we make?"

"The one who descended there," she answers.

"Jesus?"

"Yes."

"How?" I ask.

"Say this prayer," she says.

> "Jesus, make your descent
> into the hell of my compliance."

"And what will that do?"

"Just try it," she insists.

"Jesus, make your descent into the hell of my compliance."
I wait. And then, I say it again, "Jesus, make your descent into
the hell of my compliance."

A long pause . . .

> "Njeri!" I shout aloud.
> "Victim to a piece of plastic.
> I damn the house that smothered you."

> "Omondi!" I shout aloud.
> "Victim to an unwelcome microbe.
> I damn the fetid pit latrine that sickened you."

> "Maina!" I shout aloud.
> "Victim to hunger.
> I damn the *kwashiokor* that wasted you."

"It's working," Mary says. "Name the victims. And damn
the unjust conditions that cause their suffering. Keep talking,
Jesus is harrowing hell in you."

"Oh, *Dolorosa,* I want to scream. I want to cry: 'Let's spare
the children! For Christ's sake, let us spare the children!' "

"Then do so," says Mary. "It undoes hell. It deprives the devil of his martyrs. Cry out. Protest!"

"But it all seems so unreal. Please, *Dolorosa,* give me an image, a prayer story."

"Okay, imagine yourself at the public cemetery in the section for poor children, where bodies abandoned at the hospital are dumped together in a mass grave. You are there alone in the late afternoon."

"Yes, and I have three things with me: a Bible, a rosary, and a silver container."

"Fine. So what would you do?"

"I would open the Bible and pray the following passages":

> I have looked away, and kept silence,
> I have said nothing, holding myself in;
> but now, I cry out as a woman in labor,
> gasping and panting.
> > Isaiah 42:14

> I will not restrain my tongue:
> in my anguish of spirit I will speak,
> in my bitterness of soul I shall complain.
> > Job 7:11

> For I am filled with misery,
> my life is on the brink of Sheol;
> left alone among the dead,
> like the slaughtered lying in the grave.
> > Psalm 88:3, 5

> O that my head were waters,
> and my eyes a fountain of tears

> that I might weep day and night
> for the slain of the daughter of my people.
> Jeremiah 9:1

> For Zion's sake I will not be silent,
> for Jerusalem's sake I will not be quiet,
> until her vindication shines forth like the dawn
>   and her victory like a burning torch.
> Isaiah 62:1

"I would say a rosary of requiem, a decade with each scripture; and tap the ground with every bead. Then I would tear out of the Bible the five pages with these scriptures, and place them in the silver container. Into this container I would also scoop five handfuls of dirt from the mass grave of the thrownaway children. Then I would close the container and take it to the other side of the cemetery that faces the Ngong Hills, to the tombs of the wealthy, to the tombs with permanent markers where the deceased are mourned by name. There, at last, I would bury the precious remains of the innocent dead—each of whom has a name repeated by God's angel, a name that echoes in heaven and in hell.

"Then I would address myself to the mother I misadvised:

> 'Hail Rachel,
> full of pain,
> the Lord is with thee.
>
> Grieved art thou among women;
> lost is the fruit of thy womb.
>
> Holy Rachel,
> mother of the massacred,
> pray for the silent
> now,
> until the hour we cry out.
>
> Amen.' "

"And if," says Mary, "passers-by witness your strange ritual
in the public cemetery, how would you explain yourself?"

"I make no apology
to those passers-by
on the sidewalk
outside the gate,
who hear me shouting
in the cemetery.

They might wonder:
what is he doing,
what business,
what shouting,
disturbing our peace?

I am here crunching the leaves underfoot.
I am here mashing the grass with my boots.
So that I might study the shifting graves,
and decry the death of the innocents.

Yes, I am here to gauge the sinking ground
that's more concave above the children's
    graves,
just to see how heavy upon them lie
the earth and we the living."

❖ 6 ❖

The Spring Journal

"I am about to return to Nairobi."

"Yes," says Mary. "So tell me, what have you learned during this year of reflection?"

"I understand now what is required of me. I will never allow another child to die. I will take control of the situation when I get back to Africa. I'll be busier than ever. You'll see."

"You have it all wrong!" Mary exclaims. "Hyperactivity is another form of numbing yourself, another way of muting your sorrow. And listen," Mary says, "it is not for you to take control of the situation. That is patronizing."

"Then tell me," I ask, "what is the work I am to do?"

"Be a mentor of defiance!" Mary says. "Help others in the same way that I helped Jesus through the phases of grief, in the same way that I helped him to lament and to defy. You must teach those tempted to resignation to feel, to cry out, to work for change."

"How?" I ask.

"Stop protecting people! Stop patronizing them. Let them feel their grief."

I stand up, agitated.

"Sit down!" she says. "I'm telling you this, and in strong language, because I do not want you to speak to my people in the voice of the Silencer. I do not want you to spread 'occupation philosophy.' You are a minister in the religion of defiance, not the religion of hell."

I imagine the passionate, wide-open eyes of Mary. I hear fire in her voice as she continues: "Do you understand me? I want you to harrow the hell around you! Break the silence. Let people lament. And their grief, the grief of the oppressed, will produce change."

"How so?"

"Think back over this year," Mary says. "How has grief changed you? Think about your year-long meditation. How did grief change Jesus? What does it supply?"

"Courage."

"Yes," says Mary. "Don't get me wrong. The mere shedding of tears is not what I advocate. Rather, wet-eyed, raise defiant hands and grasp the lever of history. Yank on it."

"And is that the Marian mission?" I ask.

"Yes!" she says. "Shut down every social system that slaughters the innocent."

I visualized Mary's jaw, that thermometer of her conviction, being out as far as it could go.

"Do you know the surest proof of the existence of God?" says she.

"No," I answer. "What is the surest proof of the existence of God?"

"An outraged mother," says Mary.

She takes a deep breath. "Yes! That's the surest proof of the existence of God."

There is a long pause.

"Where," she continues, "do you think these feelings of outrage come from? Why does a person get fed up and say, 'Never again!' Why do some people risk their lives to put down the mighty from their thrones and uplift the lowly?"

"I don't know."

"Because," says Mary, "God's outraged spirit is moving them to do these things. They are manifesting the defiance of God."

"An epiphany!" I say.

"Yes," says Mary, "defiance is epiphany—one of the ways God reveals God's own self in the world.

"The defiant one names the child she loses to malnutrition. She buries the child. She grieves for the child. Then she works to change the system; she demands jobs for women.

"The defiant one names her infant who dies during delivery. She buries the child. She grieves for the child. Then she works to change the system; she demands proper medical treatment for pregnant women.

"The defiant one names her aborted child, repenting of what she did. She buries the child. She grieves for the child. Then she works to change the system; she demands nonviolent alternatives for women in crisis pregnancies."

There is a very long pause. I listen for more.

"As a missionary," says Mary, "you might think that you bring people the revelation of God. That's not true. You call it out of people. You help people feel God move in them. You help people experience God's passion for justice. And then *they* reveal God in acts of holy defiance.''

Our conversation is over. I imagine Mary standing before me. I kneel. I imagine her stretching out her hands. She places her palms firmly on my head. And she commissions me.

I am now ready to go back to Africa. I pledge myself to the Marian mission with these words addressed to Mama Njeri, Mama Omondi, and Mama Maina:

> "Raw and salty, Rachel,
> let roll tears of outrage.
>
> In a better world than this,
> your child would never die thus.
>
> Cry out, Rachel, raise your fist,
> worry not 'tis blasphemous.
>
> Against God you raise it not;
> for God's the one most put out.
>
> It's God's clenched fist you extend
> and a screaming God questions:
>
> 'Why is it that I'm abandoned?'
> And like you God hears no answer.
>
> But I tell you, Rachel, sing;
> rout despair a-festering.
>
> Sing, Rachel, sing, make merry;
> sting grinning fatality.

Wipe its foolish grin away;
nobler humor wins the day.

The gardener's in disguise;
look, the undertaker lies.

Christ risen opens every grave
and commands our dead, 'Yield not!'

So, defiant Rachel, sing!
Sing, sorrowing mother, sing!''

III

A Companion
on Journeys
and
in Journals

Preface

In the autumn, winter, and spring journals I discovered an interesting development. The question I asked of suffering changed. In the beginning I asked why. But one doesn't get far asking that question of suffering. So I began, in Marian fashion, to ask suffering a question it could answer — how?

The winter journal is filled with splotches of ink from times of anger when I pressed down too hard on the pen; every other page has a messy scrawl, indecipherable, the tracks of some emotional animal rampaging the notebook. The spring journal has fewer splotches, less mess. Letters and words stand erect and firm. The grief changed! Gone is the seething and sentiment. There is more decision. There is more resolution. And there are plans. In the spring journal there are pages of ideas about how my community and I could address the causes of suffering.

In the autumn, winter, and spring journals I recognized a development Dorothee Soelle describes as "phases" in her book *Suffering*. I call them the three phases of grief: silence, lamentation, and defiance. In the first phase one is speechless, isolated, dominated by the situation. In the second phase one groans, like the psalmist, and begins to analyze the situation, "With my harp I shall solve the riddle." In the third phase one makes plans, organizes, and, in solidarity with others, shapes the situation.

On my journeys and in my journals I met a companion: *Mater Dolorosa,* Mother of the Defiant. She is a companion in ministry. She walks with every apostle. She guides us through the phases of apostolic grief from lamentation to defiance. Mary understands apostolic sorrow. She had a good share of it in her own life. The Spirit often groaned within her. She lamented. The sorrow of the *Mater Dolorosa,* however, must not be mistaken for depression. Holy sorrow is very different from depression. By their fruits you know the difference.

Holy sorrow is like the blues. James Cone in *The Spirituals and the Blues* says:

> There was no attempt to evade the reality of suffering. Black slaves faced the reality of the world "ladened with trouble, an' burden'd wid grief," but they believed that they could go to Jesus in secret and get relief. They appealed to Jesus not so much to remove the trouble (though that was included), but to keep them from "sinkin' down."

> Oh, Lord, Oh, My Lord!
> Oh, My Good Lord! Keep me from sinkin' down.
> Oh, Lord, Oh, My Lord!
> Oh, My Good Lord! Keep me from sinkin' down.

The black American religious experience expressed in the spirituals can help Catholics appreciate their own religious experience of the Mother of Sorrows. Hymns to the *Mater Dolorosa,* what I call the Catholic blues, prepare the heart for Kingdom hope. A spiritual that begins "I am a poor pilgrim of sorrow" continues,

> Sometimes I'm tossed and driven.
> Sometimes I don't know where to roam.
> I've heard of a city called heaven.
> I've started to make it my home.

Lamentation ends and defiance begins when one decides to live "as if." Making heaven home, "as if" living, is an act of holy defiance. Without denying present reality, one lives as if in tomorrow, as if the Day of the Lord has come: the ultimate reality. "As if" thinking makes Kingdom workers bold.

> If I had-a my way,
> If I had-a my way, little children,
> If I had-a my way,
> I'd tear this building down.
> Great God, then, if I had-a my way,
> If I had-a my way, little children,
> If I had-a my way,
> I'd tear this building down.

Holy sorrow, then, leads to holy defiance. "But what's that?" asked one reader of my manuscript. "Tell me," she said, "what does the defiant one do?"

The defiant one acts like the *Mater Dolorosa*. The defiant one helps others to feel their grief and then to use their grief as a power source for change. The defiant one helps the oppressed to name injustice and to tear down structures that massacre the innocent.

But defiance is not only tearing down. It takes more defiance to build up, to build up communities whose mission is to oppose the sinister power of cynicism that grips our world.

Defiant ones establish defiant communities that cry out, "No, this ought not to be; we will not let this be!" Such communities can breach the wall of indifference that surrounds so many modern hearts.

Mary is the standard bearer for defiant communities. She leads them in projects that raise up the lowly, projects that empower the poor to smash such ancient foes as hunger. Hunger ought not to be, and the family of Mary will not let it be!

After my journeys and journals I had better eyes for spotting the *Mater Dolorosa,* Mother of the Defiant. I began to see her at work in the world. What follows are "snapshots" of Mary walking with the apostles of Jesus on their journey through grief to defiance.

❖ 7 ❖

Mary, *Mater Dolorosa*

The Age of Antigone

It has been said that prior to the Second Vatican Council the church emphasized Good Friday too much. Today, the church is rightfully putting more emphasis on Easter Sunday.

What I believe the pre–Vatican II and post–Vatican II church have both neglected, however, is Holy Saturday. And it is a pity, because Holy Saturday is the time in which we are living. At the end of the twentieth century, after the Calvary of numerous wars and famines, we find ourselves at the tomb.

Look at Armenia, Northern Ireland, and South Africa. The most impassioned social protests at the end of the twentieth century take place at funerals. Huge crowds are drawn to graveside demonstrations. What does this say about the times in which we are living?

The sixties was the age of Aquarius. The nineties, I believe, is the age of Antigone. Her story is a paradigm for people today.

In this classic Greek tragedy, Antigone, a daughter of Oedipus, wants to provide the proper funeral rites for Polynices, her dead brother. But their uncle Creon, the tyrant who killed Polynices, has passed a law against such a burial. Antigone's sister Ismene questions her plans.

Ismene:	But defy the city? I have no strength for that.
Antigone:	You have your excuses. I am on my way, I'll raise a mound for him, for my dear brother.
Ismene:	Oh Antigone, you're so rash—I'm so afraid for you!
Antigone:	Don't fear for me. Set your own life in order.
Ismene:	Then don't, at least, blurt this out to anyone. Keep it a secret. I'll join you in that, I promise.
Antigone:	Dear god, shout it from the rooftops. I'll hate you all the more for silence—tell the world!

Antigone buries Polynices. Creon becomes outraged. To the despot, burying the dead is an act of rebellion. The sorrow of Antigone is subversive.

After the atrocities suffered by children in two world wars, at Auschwitz, and in Vietnam, it is time for crying out and for outrage. After the atrocities suffered by children in the famines of Bangladesh, Kampuchea, Biafra, the Sahel, Ethiopia, Sudan, Somalia, and Mozambique, it is time for lamentation and defiance. At the end of this bloody twentieth century it is time to bury the dead.

Jesus wants the living, those who demand justice, to bury the dead. Their sorrow is a righteous passion that must be released.

This chapter presents some prayers and poems that have helped bereft people to release their sorrow. With the *Mater Dolorosa* as mentor, they have made their way through lamentation and have reached the threshold of defiance.

Stabat Mater Dolorosa in the Twelfth Century

Jacopone da Todi was born in 1235 and died in 1306. He was passionately devoted to his wife. She was everything to him.

Sport was the next most important thing in Jacopone da Todi's life. He loved going to tournaments and watching knights in combat. One day in 1268 he took his wife to a popular tournament. It was very crowded, but they managed to obtain good seats in the grandstand. Then something happened that changed Jacopone da Todi's life. The grandstand collapsed, killing his beloved wife.

Jacopone was overwhelmed. He gave up his wealth and home and wandered the countryside as a poor beggar. He felt numb inside and empty.

Then in 1290 Jacopone entered the Franciscans. This was a turning point. He began to express his grief by writing poems.

> At the cross her station keeping
> Stood the mournful Mother weeping,
>   Where he hung, the dying Lord;
> For her soul, of joy bereaved,
> Bowed with anguish, deeply grieved,
>   Felt the sharp and piercing sword.
>
> O how sad and sore distressed
> Now was she, that Mother blessed
>   Of the Sole begotten One!
> Deep the woe of her affliction,
> When she saw the crucifixion
>   Of her ever-glorious Son.
>
> Who, on Christ's dear Mother gazing
> Pierced by anguish so amazing,
>   Born of woman, would not weep?
> Who, on Christ's dear Mother thinking
> Such a cup of sorrow drinking,
>   Would not share her sorrows deep?
>
> For his people's sins chastised,
> She beheld her Son despised,
>   Scourged, and crowned with thorns
>   entwined;

Saw him then from judgment taken,
And in death by all forsaken,
   Till his spirit he resigned.

O good Jesu, let me borrow
Something of thy Mother's sorrow,
   Fount of love, Redeemer kind,
That my heart fresh ardor gaining,
And a purer love attaining,
   May with thee acceptance find.

Stabat Mater Dolorosa in the Nineteenth Century

Antonin Dvorak was born in 1841 and died in 1904. He studied music in Prague and played his viola in the orchestra of the National Theater. Brahms discovered him in 1875 and helped Antonin get a job composing for the Austrian emperor's minister of culture.

Then misfortune struck. In September 1875 Antonin's first child died. To express his emotional pain he composed a setting for Jacopone da Todi's "Stabat Mater." Antonin sketched the score between February 19 and May 7, 1876, and put it on a shelf.

In August and September of the following year Antonin lost two more children. Disconsolate, he returned to the shelf and took up the score again. He finished it on November 13, 1877. It was first performed in Prague on December 23, 1880.

Antonin Dvorak conducted his "Stabat Mater" in England on several occasions. Though it was sung in Latin, the translation of the text was given in print. The following verses, a piece of Antonin Dvorak's rendition of da Todi's poem, convey a darker hue of grief and a more insistent appeal for the gift of tears.

The mourning mother stood weeping by the
   cross
from which her son was hung.

Her heaving soul, sad and laden with grief,
was pierced by the sword. . . .

Who would not weep at the sight of Christ's
  mother
in such a torment? . . .

Loving mother, fount of love, make me feel
  thy grief,
that I mourn with thee. . . .

Let me weep with thee. . . .

I long to stand with thee at the cross,
and mourn with thee.

Virgin of Virgins, be not against me now;
  share thy tears with me.

Stabat Mater Dolorosa in the Twentieth Century

According to UNICEF, forty thousand children die every day
from malnutrition and preventable diseases. Let us pray . . .

I am brother *doloroso*.
I am sister *dolorosa*.
Yes, I am shouting
  to the *Mater Dolorosa* . . .

"Hail Mary, full of grace,
Pray for the human race

To end all fear, war, and greed
The forty thousand to feed.

Blessed are you among women
Help us, every woman and man

To become the fruit of thy womb,
An advocate of children, as

Jesus.

Holy Mary, Mother of God,
Pray we spread defiance.

Now,
Until the children are fed.
Amen.''

Hymns for the Holy Innocents in the Fifth Century

On December 28, the Feast of the Holy Innocents, the church for many centuries sang the following hymn of Prudentius (348-413) at Matins.

With terror doth the tyrant hear
The King of kings hath come to dwell,
Where David's court shall widely rear,
A sceptered reign o'er Israel.

Then cries out, raging, at the word:
"He comes to stand where we have stood:
Hence, soldier, and with ruthless sword
Deluge the cradles deep with blood!"

What availeth so great an outrage?

Hymns for the Holy Innocents in the Twentieth Century

Ann and Jim Clune have opened their home to homeless people in Binghamton, New York, for the last twenty years.

They and their six children welcome the needy person into what they call a "Christ room," a place where they would have liked to welcome Jesus if they had been residents of Bethlehem when his family was looking for lodging two thousand years ago.

It is not only December 25 and the role of the innkeeper that Ann and Jim Clune reenact. They also reenact December 28 and the role of Rachel. The Clunes commemorate the Feast of the Holy Innocents every year by pointing out the Herod of today who threatens our children with nuclear war.

Their "pointing out" takes different forms. Most of the time they stay in upstate New York, where they stand in silent vigil on some frigid street corner in front of institutions that manufacture machines for war or recruit volunteers for war.

One year they took their message to Washington. They stood in front of the River Entrance to the Pentagon and made a vow of nonviolence. They sealed the vow by painting a cross on the steps there using a small vial of their own blood.

The poem below was written by Ann Clune and was recited that day at the Pentagon. It expresses the sorrow she feels for the victims of military atrocities and then proclaims the Marian "NO!" With Ann's poem we make the transition from sorrow to defiance.

> Herod! It is in vain
>   you spill our children's blood.
> What violence seems to gain
>   can never last for good.
>
> Herod! This killing is futile.
>   It cannot secure your power.
> Don't you see death can't touch this Child
>   before his appointed hour?
>
> And when that hour comes
>   and his blood is willingly shed,

You must see that it's his life that triumphs
and your power that dies instead.

Herod! Your spirit's continued
for too many hundreds of years,
To grow by nourishing hatreds,
continually feeding our fears.

Herod, you have governed
in so very many nations,
Threatening and carrying out
the worst abominations.

For too long now good people have watched
your power growing here,
Though we may weep and mourn,
we'll no longer wait in fear.

For Herod! We have a King
who's greater than you by far!
He'll give us the strength to confront you
both here and wherever you are.

Herod! We're here to shout NO!
to the evil you'd do in our names.
The power you seek still eludes you,
and your threats and your crimes are in vain.

NO! Herod! We'll not be a part of your fear
and your power-hungry will.
In Jesus' name we now promise that our own
is the only blood we will spill.

Mary, Mentor of the Defiant

Atrocity and Apparition

Pilgrims have been coming to Medjugorje, Croatia, since 1981, the year six children of that now famous town reported seeing apparitions of Mary, the Mother of God. The seers continue to report having the experience, now on a daily basis, and now with a name: The Queen of Peace.

A little known fact about the reported apparitions of Mary at Medjugorje is that they began on a hill very close to the site of an infamous World War II massacre.

Croatian Catholics in the vicinity herded Orthodox Serbians to the brow of a very steep cliff just outside Medjugorje. There the Croatians threw the Serbians to their death hundreds of feet below. Scores of innocent civilians were killed that day.

The hill of the reported apparitions is practically within sight of the hill of the massacre. It is there that the children heard a message of penance and conversion.

My own interpretation of these events is that Mary of Medjugorje is the Mary of this book, the woman who experienced the slaughter of the innocents, the mother of sorrow and defiance.

What is the message of the Croatian children? They say that

Mary wants them to tell the people of Medjugorje, the progeny of the perpetrators of the atrocity, to do penance and be converted.

This should not surprise us. Mary did the same thing in her lifetime. She raised up a child to confront the progeny of the one who slew the innocents. She raised up Jesus to bring down the mighty from their thrones.

The message of Medjugorje is that we should become like Jesus—nonviolent prophets who confront the perpetrators of atrocity and who call them to repentance. (Perhaps if the message had been heeded the world would have been spared the terrible brutalities of the Yugoslav civil war.)

The Queen of Peace raises us up to bring down the mighty idol of war. The spirit of Mary takes us, like the Croatian children, to the site of slaughter and teaches us the necrology of "never again."

Mary appears not only in Medjugorje; she is appearing in Sudan, and in Somalia (where 20 percent of the children under five are reported to have starved to death in the first six months of 1992). Mary appears in every place where she wants the innocents remembered. Wherever children suffer, the defiant mother appears to lay bare what is covered, to declare what is hushed. She may look like the Pieta, or she may act like Antigone, but she always appears to disrupt the silence, to disturb the compliant with her brave bereavement and her repeated demands to end atrocity.

The Silencer wants us to look away from the apparition. He fears the one who would mentor us in defiance; he is no match for the one who harrows hell on earth. Mary persistently appears at the site of massacre because she wants to make it clear that the innocent dead have a mother and a name . . . and a right to judge us if we remain silent.

A Doctor's Defiance

There was a doctor in Africa who cared for a minority ethnic group. She struggled for many years to change the deplorable health conditions in one isolated and remote village. She educated the parents about immunization, about oral rehydration therapies for intestinal diarrheal diseases, and about other aspects of nutrition and sanitation. The health of the villagers slowly improved. More children were surviving. People lived longer.

The government soldiers had always disliked these villagers because they belonged to the same ethnic group as members of a guerrilla movement. One day, several government soldiers were ambushed and killed by the guerrillas. Companions of the dead soldiers directed their revenge at the villagers, though the villagers had had nothing to do with the ambush.

It happened in the morning. A group of government soldiers entered the village. Using automatic weapons, they opened fire on the unarmed civilians. Even the children were not spared. The banging of the guns and the pleading of the mothers created a sinister cacophony.

The doctor, hearing the commotion, went quickly to the scene of the massacre. The soldiers had just jumped into their jeeps and were off. She surveyed the carnage.

Bodies were strewn everywhere: in the doorways of cottages, in the playground of the school, in front of the childcare clinic, near the community well. Some people were dead; others were still alive. Bodies that she had mended and mothered were now dead or writhing in pain.

Immediately the doctor tended the wounded. She stopped their bleeding. She made them comfortable. She gave directions to the nursing attendants concerning the program of care required for each patient.

Then the doctor got into her jeep. She began to collect the bodies of the dead. She drove by the doorways of the cottages, by the playground of the school, by the front of the childcare clinic, by the community well. One by one she hoisted the bodies up into her arms and momentarily held them to her breast, remembering this or that episode of illness in their life when she had healed them. Each corpse was reverently placed on the floor of the back of the jeep.

Then she drove to a town a few miles away where the office of the regional administrator was located. Each trip to the town the doctor carried five bodies. There, at the front steps of the administrator's office, she arranged the bodies. She carefully positioned them in such a way that it appeared they were registering a complaint with the government. In this way she knit the two spots together — the scene of the slaughter and the government office — so that no one would mistake the government's link in this massacre. She literally laid the blame at their door.

The doctor was arrested. But this only gave the incident wider publicity. Eventually, an investigation was called for.

Thus the doctor, in this true story, harrowed the hell around her. She did not surrender the victims of the slaughter to the Silencer. Even in death they witnessed to life, to the reverence for life that is due every human being. Even as corpses they defied their executioners; they would not allow the massacre to communicate a lesson of submission to survivors.

"Through death they render powerless him who had the power of death, that is, the devil; and deliver those who through fear of death were subject to slavery all their lives" (Hebrews 2:14, 15).

Expectant Mothers

In 1985 I was working with young people in a squatter neighborhood in East Nairobi. To get there I had to cross the Nairobi River on a foot bridge. One day midway on the bridge I chanced to see in the river, caught in an eddy of rocks, a small plastic bag. I climbed down to the water's edge and poked the bag with a stick. Out spilled a baby.

Sick to my stomach I walked a few more yards into the neighborhood. I asked the people there about my discovery.

They informed me that someone a few houses away carried on an abortion business. This surprised me, because I had never come across such a thing in rural Africa. Nairobi, however, was quite a Westernized city. I wondered what I should do.

Knowing the person involved, I decided to go visit her. I took with me a small booklet that showed how a baby develops in the womb. "What makes you do this?" I asked her. She said that she needed the money. "But what about the children?" And I showed her the booklet. She got angry. She repeated that she needed the money, and she didn't care whom she hurt to get it.

I went back to the Marianist residence, sat down in the chapel, and prayed. "What would you want to have happen?" I asked God. I decided that I would try to become a friend of this abortionist.

I returned to her home the next week and the week after. Every week for a year I went back, until, indeed, we did become friends. During these weekly visits she told me about herself, and I told her about myself. We talked about life and about compassion and about Jesus. We even prayed together.

One day she asked me to leave the now familiar booklet on prenatal development with her. The brightness in her eyes told me that she had been visited by grace. Shortly after this she joined a catechism class and was baptized.

Things changed after that. When customers approached this now converted abortionist, she would show them that booklet and say, "I don't want to take the life of your child. But I want to help. What can I do to help?" She spent hours talking with women. Sometimes she even took one in and housed her for the duration of the pregnancy. At some point she would say, "Why don't you also go to see Brother Peter?"

And they did. A line of expectant mothers formed one day in front of the Marianist residence. They asked the brother who answered the door if they all could see Peter.

I said a quick prayer, "God, show me what you want to

happen now." I led the women into the living room. We sat down together and talked. One woman said, "I have no alternative. I don't have a husband. How can I make it on my own? I'm alone. What can I do?"

Then another woman responded, "No! You're not alone. You have me and all your sisters here! Let's keep meeting every week, and let's keep talking until we find a solution." The others unanimously agreed.

Thus the women met weekly and discussed their hopes, fears, and dreams. They shared Gospel stories. Their favorite one was the visitation. "Look," they said, "Mary had an unexpected pregnancy. What did she do? She went to be with another woman who also had an unexpected pregnancy. That's what we're doing."

The group relished the parallel. They said, "What did those two women with unexpected pregnancies talk about when they came together at Elizabeth's hut? St. Luke tells us they talked about changes, yes, they talked about changes needed in the world. They talked about bringing down the mighty 'Bwana' from their thrones. They talked about lifting up the lowly 'maskini.' They said that the rich should disappear and that the hungry are to eat."

"And now," the group of expectant mothers asked themselves, "aren't these the same kind of changes we want in our city?"

I asked them, "What specific changes would make a difference in your lives? What kind of changes would make a better future for you and your children?"

The reply was instant and unequivocal. To a woman they all said, "JOBS! EMPLOYMENT! WE WANT TO WORK!"

Thus Maria House began. It was born of a group of expectant mothers. These defiant women wanted a chance to start again, or to put it more precisely, they wanted to be given their first chance. They wanted one decent break. They wanted one good try at making life work. And they got it! Or rather, they

created it. When given two choices, they took the third! They invented a possibility.

Eight years later, through the Maria House Program, hundreds of other women have also taken that chance at making life work. Pregnant and alone, a woman finds support at Maria House from peers who are in similar circumstances. They meet and talk every week. Then at the time of delivery she is given part of the hospital fee and clothes for the newborn. When the baby is six months old, the mother begins a course in a manufacturing trade. One year later she is ready to work. Maria House is involved with that step too. It helps her to find a job or to open her own business.

The original group of expectant single mothers at Maria House used to pray their own creed. This creed has been handed down from one group to the next and is the first prayer the newcomers learn. The women's weekly support meetings always end with the resolution not to believe the lies others spread about them, and the single mother's creed: *"Nina imani katika Mungu ambaye ana imani katika mimi."* ("I believe in the God who believes in me.")

The Defiant

What is defiance? Or, rather, what is it not?

Being defiant is not the same as being obstinate. Saying no for the wrong reasons is just willfulness. A chip on the shoulder is not defiance. It's defensiveness. Nor is being defiant the same as being violent.

How then can defiance be described? What does it look like? It is simply standing up for what matters. It looks like that rural doctor and those expectant mothers. They had Mary's determined jaw.

It looks like Rosa Parks. On December 1, 1955, she was asked by a bus driver in Montgomery, Alabama, to surrender her seat to a white man. She was tired. She just said, "No."

And she added, "Why should I have to get up and stand? Why should we have to be pushed around?" Mild-mannered and soft-spoken, Rosa Parks launched the Civil Rights Movement by sitting down for what matters.

Defiance looks like Dorothy Day. One day in the early fifties, she sat down on a bench in New York City's Central Park and refused to take shelter during an air raid drill. She just said, "No." It wasn't right to comply. "We were setting our faces against things as they are . . . against war and getting ready for war." She was practically alone in the beginning. In a few years, however, thousands were sitting on Central Park benches, listening to the air raid siren blaring and not heeding its demands. The frustrated Civil Defense authorities finally decided to drop the air raid drills in New York City.

Defiance looks like Candy Lightner—a Los Angeles mother. One day in 1980 her daughter Cari was walking to school in the bicycle lane. The car of a drunk driver careened over the curb, proceeded down the bicycle path, and hit and killed Cari instantly. The car then sped away. The guilty driver was apprehended. He had already been arrested five times before for drunk driving, but he had never lost his license! In 1980 the courts did not take drunk driving very seriously. But Candy Lightner did! She fought the courts. She demanded change. She founded MADD—Mothers Against Drunk Driving. Candy Lightner just said, "No." She said no to twenty-three thousand people (five thousand of whom are children) losing their lives every year in alcohol-related car accidents in the United States. Her organization has succeeded in having hundreds of new laws enacted against drunk driving. Thousands of lives are saved every year thanks to these new laws.

No is a very Marian word. This surprises people who always associate Mary with *fiat,* which they say means acceptance, even compliance.

Where in the Gospel does Mary say no?

She says no during the visitation to her cousin Elizabeth,

when Mary sings the Magnificat. In that bold proclamation Mary says no to the mighty on their thrones (maybe that is why John, who would later confront Herod, leapt in his mother's womb). She says no to the well-fed. She says no to the oppressor who exploits the poor and the hungry. That is how holy defiance works.

Rosa Parks, Dorothy Day, and Candy Lightner exercised leadership by using the Marian no. One determined person can make a difference!

One does not get defiant about a lot of things. Maybe there are only two or three things that truly merit defiance. Those two or three things matter. For those things one is willing to die. So one takes a stand and doesn't budge. Like the Chinese student of the Tiananmen Square uprising who placed himself in front of a line of tanks, one says, "No, I will not allow this thing past me."

❖ 9 ❖

I See Beauty Before Me

In the Sahel with No Heaven

November 5, 1975, is the first time I encountered a grieving mother. I was a Peace Corps Volunteer in Keita, a remote village in the Sahelien country of Niger in West Africa. The mother was a middle-aged Hausa who lived on a principal lane of the village. I occasionally met this woman if I passed her house when I was out walking.

On November 3 I was walking past her house, and the woman stopped me. She invited me into her compound and handed me her baby daughter.

The child was underweight and breathing irregularly. The mother told me that the child had diarrhea and vomited whatever she ate.

When I held the child in my hands, I touched each of her ribs with my fingers. She looked up. Without crying, the baby gazed at me with large, sunken eyes. She had the wizened expression of an old woman. Her cheekbones dominated her face.

For the next two days the nurse at the village clinic treated the child, but the clinic lacked the intravenous drip the child needed. The little girl died on November 5.

I saw the mother holding the deceased child when I arrived at her house. Hundreds of thousands of people had already perished from the Sahelien drought. The famine was real to me now. That statistic had the face of a seven-month-old infant.

I stared at her tiny body. I thought about the weather. What a cruel coincidence that this child died just before the harvest. The drought had ended several months ago—with the return of the seasonal rains. This mother must have carried her lifeless child home from the clinic through fields of high-standing millet.

Still staring at the tiny body of this infant I began to daydream. I remembered an incident that happened just before this baby was born.

It was the first day of the rainy season. I saw the dark sky open and the refreshing coolness pour down. I breathed in deeply. Nothing in all the world smells sweeter than wet desert air. Then I saw them.

Every house opened and out poured children. They met the sky. With mouths opened they tasted the spring rains. And then they ran straight for the first puddles, thrilled to the toes. With the rain still coming down, the children danced naked in the year's first puddles. The delight in their faces was so concentrated that it seemed like ecstasy.

Remembering those puddles made the silence grow heavy.

The woman was looking at me. I sensed that she wanted me to say something, something consoling. I thought: "Am I to make sense of such a damn stupid death? Does she want me to speak about heaven? And what if I speak about heaven? How will heaven talk affect the way she sees this thing and her motivation to change what she does not like about the world? Speaking about heaven will make her more resigned. I won't do it."

That was my way of thinking when I was young and understood neither grief nor heaven.

Heart of a Heartless World

In my youth I resisted heaven. Though not a Marxist, I sympathized with some of Marx's ideas.

Religion is the sigh of the oppressed creature, the heart of a heartless world, just as it is the spirit of an unspiritual situation. It is the opium of the people.

The abolition of religion as the illusory happiness of the people is required for their real happiness. The demand to give up the illusions . . . is the demand to give up a condition which needs illusions.

I had no quarrel with the Gospel of liberation. I wanted to be a Christian. Heaven was the problem. I thought it a cowardly notion. It prevented the elimination of miserable conditions on earth that were disguised by heavenly illusions. So I thought in my twenties.

Remembering the dead fired up my defiance. I banished the thought of them in heaven. I believed that picturing them in paradise would undermine my passion for justice. After a few years, however, I discovered that this attitude wore me out. I was still outraged, but now I was outraged and tired.

Notions for Nausea

There is an event from my childhood that Marx would not have approved of. Whenever I got sick to my stomach, whatever time of day or night, and was vomiting into the toilet bowl, my mother would appear beside me. She would put her right hand across my forehead and hold me up with her left hand, bracing me at the waist. And all the while I was heaving and distressed, my mother would say, "Think of Christmas."

She did the same thing, invoking the same image, whenever

I fell down, or cut myself, or was hurting in some way.

"Heaven," I told my mother when I was an adolescent, "is an opiate for the oppressed." I told her that it would be better not to mention it to poor people. That way their anger would well up to a revolutionary explosion. And this explosion would demolish unjust social structures. "Don't give them pie in the sky," I would say. "Deal with the facts and be a realist."

This is the way I thought before I started working with poor people. Now my experience tells me something different. Now I see that there was something profound in my mother's approach to pain and suffering. Over the long haul, people in any sort of physical or mental distress become weary of suffering. The suffering becomes heavier and heavier, and by itself, it does not transform society. Rather, suffering seems to snuff out resistance. It is like snow on the new sprouts of April grass. It numbs. It immobilizes.

Suffering must be replaced by beauty.

Fix Your Attention on Beauty

After a decade of losses I found myself thinking too much about the dead as dead. The children lying in caskets, the meek expression on their faces, the carefully knit blanket cover — all this tormented me.

Often I had nightmares about children dying. In one dream I saw a child falling through a sewer grate. The bars on it were too far apart to prevent a small child from tumbling in. I tried to pull the bars together to save other children, but the heavy iron did not budge. On other nights I had a bizarre parody of Jacob's dream. But the cherubs were only descending, and many fell from the ladder. I looked everywhere for a net. I wished for the power of St. Philip Neri, who reportedly commanded a child he saw fall from a great height to stop in mid-air.

Thinking about the dead children drained my energy. I did

not imagine them as allies. They did not help me. They haunted me.

Then it happened. On April 27, 1990, I was on home-leave, driving from Pittsburgh to Mexico, New York, near Lake Ontario. I was on my way to my niece's first holy communion celebration. It was about nine o'clock in the evening, and I was listening to Handel's *Messiah*. Right after the "Alleluia Chorus" came "I know that my redeemer liveth."

And while the hymn played,

> I know that my redeemer lives;
> What joy the blest assurance gives!
> He lives, he lives, who once was dead,

they appeared.

Though I had often thought about the children, I always suffered when doing so. But as I heard the words "I know that my redeemer lives," I saw the children with Jesus. They all were splashing in puddles of the wet season's first rain. There was water everywhere, and they were singing silly songs, and they were dancing, and their eyes were bright with delight. When they finished playing, Jesus put them all into the lap of Mary. They drank from her breast. They drank and drank until they were satisifed. I overheard Mary say something to Jesus in Aramaic. I asked him what she said. He replied, "The hungry will be given good things to eat."

Shortly after this experience I was browsing through a book on Marian art. I stopped suddenly at a painting by Rubens. It was called "The Virgin in Glory with the Holy Innocents." In this painting there are forty babies (I counted them) gleefully jumping about Mary. Some are embracing each other, some are tumbling in play, but all are laughing. Their eyes are bright, and every child is fat.

"Aha," I said to myself. "Here they are again. This is what I saw in the car." And from then on, I began to experience these saints as my helpers. They taught me a lesson: the importance of visualizing the dead in glory. This made me more defiant, not less.

I realize now that being for heaven is better than being against hell. There is a time for staring down the oppressor, but it is unwise to stare too long. One can, like Ahab hunting his white whale, become obsessed with evil.

Daniel was wiser than Ahab. In the lion's den Daniel did not stare at the ferocious beasts. He turned his back on their red eyes and white teeth. Daniel looked heavenward. Evil demands our attention, because evil is vain. But, believe me, there are better things to stare at.

Like beauty.

The women in the prenatal course at Maria House have a dance. They gesture forward and say, "I see beauty before me." They gesture backward and say, "I see beauty behind me." They gesture above their heads and say, "I see beauty above me." They gesture toward the ground and say, "I see beauty below me." They turn around in a circle and say, "Look, there is beauty all around me."

That is defiance! It is saying "boo" to evil that wants so much to impress us, and "shoo" to the ugliness that tries to obsess us.

Like the saints splashing in spring puddles, these women have a message for me. In Dostoevski's words their message reads: "You shall be saved by beauty."

That is why I talk about heaven.

Words about heaven, or the *Parousia*, or the Kingdom are part of the language of defiance. Such words prevent people in pain from becoming obsessed with their suffering.

It is the true realist who invokes the image of heaven. Pain is not the final word about reality. Julian of Norwich said, "Pain is passing, bliss is lasting." This is a fact. Wallowing in thoughts about one's misery is a distortion of the facts.

Humanity, at the close of the twentieth century, is nauseated. It is heaving and distressed; it is stooping over the toilet bowl. Mary is standing beside us. She puts her right hand across our fevered brow and her left hand around our waist to brace us. And while holding us thus, she tells us: "Imagine the Magnificat world; picture the heavenly banquet where the children are given good things to eat."

"Fix your attention on such beauty," Mary continues, "and you shall bring it to earth." She insists on it, "Be defiant! Take a stand for heaven!"

> Mary, *Mater Dolorosa,*
> Walk me through gloom.
>
> Mary, Mentor of Defiance,
> Teach me your strength.
>
> Mary, Happy Queen of Heaven:
> The poor raised up!
>
> Lady of final victory:
> The hungry fed.
>
> Symbol of beauty before me,
> Increase my faith.